PERSONAL INJURY LAWSUITS

A Victim's Guide to Victory

Clayton Rawlings, Esq.

Speakeasy Publishing
73-03 Bell Blvd, #10
Oakland Gardens, NY 11364
www.speakeasypublishinginc.com

Ordering Information:

Quantity sales. Special discounts are available on quantity purchases by corporations, associations, and others. For details, contact the publisher at the address above.

Orders by U.S. trade bookstores and wholesalers. Please contact Speakeasy Publishing: Tel: (888) 991-2766 or visit www.speakeasypublishinginc.com.

Printed in the United States of America.

Published in 2018

ISBN: 978-1-946481-64-1

PREFACE

"The supreme art of war is to subdue the enemy without fighting." - Sun Tzu

"A jury consists of twelve persons chosen to decide who has the better lawyer." - Robert Frost

"When you have no basis for an argument, abuse the plaintiff." ~ Cicero, Roman politician and lawyer

"Prepare a case for settlement and you will try it, prepare a case for trial and you will settle it." - Clayton Rawlings

This is a book that explains personal injury law in conversational English. This is not a textbook for a law school, but rather an introduction to civil litigation for actual litigants. Every attempt has been made to avoid "legalese" so people with little or no legal training can understand it. No one plans or expects to be in court on a personal injury case. Then out of nowhere, life happens. The entire process can be very confusing for the uninitiated. It is my hope to pull back the curtain, so to speak, so people will not be intimidated if they find themselves thrust into, what appears to be, the very hostile environment of litigation.

Most cases are settled before trial. That said, when the other side will not be reasonable, you will find yourself in front of twelve citizens "fair and true." Keep in mind that "fair" is a relative term. One person's justice is another person's atrocity. For that reason alone, an understanding of effective litigation is crucial. It has been my experience that the public at large has no real understanding of how to resolve a lawsuit. They hear things, see things, and read things that create a belief system as to how the system works. It starts with "make a ridiculous demand and then stand on it." My favorite is "once you make a demand, they will settle. They can't afford the publicity of a trial." Nothing could be further from the truth. Litigation is controlled exclusively by the insurance carrier. They do not care one wit about what publicity will do to their insured. They just want to get out paying as little as possible and they are never afraid to litigate. They employ an army of lawyers for that very purpose.

It seems Google has made everyone a lawyer. I know this because a lot of my time is spent convincing my clients the blogger they thought was brilliant is just flat wrong. Clear your mind of so called "conventional wisdom" for a moment and read the following pages with an open mind. I am happy to take the mystery out of civil litigation in the personal injury arena so you can approach it in such a way as to maximize your recovery. Remember, the right to trial by jury is protected by the Constitution of the United States.

DEDICATION

To my wife, Deanna. Always understanding when trial went into overtime. Never angry over missed dinners, cancelled vacation, or working late into the night. The spouse of a litigator has many burdens placed upon them. None of them fair. You faced it all with grace and a smile. You took my clients' problems on as your own. For that I will be forever grateful.

ACKNOWLEDGEMENTS

It was May of 2010 when I participated in the Strategic Foresight Seminar through The University of Houston. Peter Bishop, PhD, was the director of the program and opened my eyes to the concept of "Futurism." It was Dr. Bishop who suggested I write a book on foresight and the law. It started me on the adventure of a lifetime. Twenty-four radio interviews, four books and four Hollywood screenplays later - the adventure continues. I will always be grateful to Dr. Bishop who convinced me I could write.

My entire personal injury practice was built exclusively on lawyer referrals. It was my fellow lawyers who placed their trust in me to get the job done. I will always be in debt to those who allowed me to protect those who could not protect themselves.

DISCLAIMER

This publication is intended to be used for educational purposes only. No legal advice is being given, and no attorney-client relationship is intended to be created by reading this material. The author assumes no liability for any errors or omissions or for how this book or its contents are used or interpreted or for any consequences resulting directly or indirectly from the use of this book. For legal or any other advice, please consult an experienced attorney or the appropriate expert who is aware of the specific facts of your case and is knowledgeable of the law in your jurisdiction.

Hampton & Rawlings
Personal Injury Attorneys
1927 Norfolk St
Houston, TX 77098
www.hamptonandrawlings.com
(713) 520-7701

TESTIMONIALS

"Where do I begin?!.... Clay Rawlings is one of the best, if not THE BEST! I have referred him to all my friends and family. He is a person that is very compassionate, understanding, and "there for you" when it is most needed. He has never let me down or anyone that I have referred. He is not just a fabulous person but a remarkable one as well. His work ethics and attention to detail are impeccable. There are not many attorneys that will go the extra mile for their client as Clay has. I am forever thankful to Clay Rawlings and he will always get referrals from me!"

Michael Pieniuta

A Satisfied Client

"I have referred all my personal injury cases to Clay Rawlings for over 25 years and he never let me down. Clay is the most tenacious personal injury attorney I know, and what a superb brilliant legal mind he has. There are very few attorneys that ever reach his caliber, yet he is humble and a natural mentor. It is a true honor and privilege to work with him, and watch him work his magic in a courtroom."

Stephen K. Leatherman

Attorney at Law

Houston, Texas

"I have known Clay Rawlings for over 30 years and have had the honor of assisting him in mediating cases I have referred to him. Clay approaches mediation as if he were trying a case to a jury. When he addresses the opposition, they are overwhelmed with the evidence and the visual aids he has prepared. I watched him go after a slumlord who allowed his properties to fall into such disrepair a young mentally-ill girl lost her life in a fire. The slumlord's bravado quickly melted when he realized Clay had found his numerous properties and would take them all to pay for the young girl's loss of life. He forced the slumlord to pay a substantial settlement out of his own personal funds because he had no insurance. But that was not enough for Clay. He also required the slumlord to place fire detectors in all his properties as a condition of the settlement. This only happens when you come to mediation so prepared the other side realizes a trial would inevitably lead to a large jury verdict."

James Randall Smith

Attorney at Law

"I've known Clay Rawlings for 35 years and I have tried cases with him as well as against him. Clay is the lawyer's lawyer in personal injury and I hold his legal acumen in the highest esteem. He possesses an exceptional understanding of people, the law and the Court. Clay couples an unparalleled trial experience with an uncanny ability to read the essential elements of any case, whether witnesses, damages, facts or theory. In short, he's a damn good lawyer!"

Michael Peck

Attorney at Law

TABLE OF CONTENTS

ABOUT THE AUTHOR

I received my undergraduate degree in 1977 from the University of Texas. I then graduated from The University of Houston Law School with a JD in 1980. I have been a licensed attorney ever since and have spent my entire 39 years in litigation. I have tried to verdict over 150 cases. Starting as an Assistant District Attorney for Harris County, Texas, I handled everything from auto theft to capital murder. I left the DA's office in 1985 and with my partner, Keith Hampton, we formed Hampton & Rawlings. We started as a criminal defense firm for the first six years. In 1991 I tried my first personal injury case and obtained a jury verdict of $1,061,000. We then spent the next 28 years focused primarily on obtaining economic justice for the injured and disabled. Since that time, Hampton & Rawlings has recovered many millions of dollars on behalf of our clients. It has been my honor to serve with my partner, Keith Hampton, for 34 years.

I am married to the love of my life and we have raised 5 wonderful children who are all educated and raising families of their own. My oldest son owns a very successful barbershop in Santa Monica, California. My youngest daughter won the silver medal in the NCWA finals and was declared an All American. She was the first female wrestler to ever represent The University of Texas. My second youngest daughter is in an artillery unit in the United States Army. She is presently assigned as a gunner on a multi rocket launcher and her unit is about to deploy to Afghanistan. They have been assigned as support for an elite Rangers Unit. I am proud of all my children. I raised my girls to be warriors. It never occurred to me they would take it literally.

I have always been a thrill seeker. For that reason I have been a downhill snow skier, scuba diver (including wreck, cave, and night dives), and skydiver. I flew with the Texas Air Aces and engaged in mock aerial combat at 10,000 feet. I parachuted twice from 13,000 feet. My wife and I have run with the bulls in Pamplona, Spain three times. Nearly gored twice. We returned to Texas, bruised, bloodied, but head unbowed. It is that same sense of adventure that I take into the courtroom.

CHAPTER 1

DEFINITION OF A TORT

It is important to understand where liability comes from. The technical term for a personal injury case is a tort. The term "tort" means a wrongful act or infringement of a right, leading to civil liability. There are four elements that must exist for a tort to be actionable: duty, breach of duty, causation, and injury. In order to claim damages, there must be a breach of the duty of the defendant towards the plaintiff, which results in an injury. The three main types of torts are negligence, strict liability (product liability), and intentional torts.

For example, when operating a motor vehicle, you have a duty to the public to operate your vehicle in a reasonable and prudent fashion. This would include obeying all traffic signals. If you run a red light, that is negligence. You have violated a duty you have to the public. If you strike another vehicle and injure someone, then your negligence caused the injury and you are responsible for all the damages the other driver has sustained. It is no more complicated than that example. Duty, breach, causation, and damages are what defines a tort.

Strict liability comes into play on product liability cases for design defects or a manufacturer's failure to warn. They have put a dangerous product or drug into the stream of commerce and are now liable to those who were injured.

An intentional tort is one where you intended for things to happen. An assault would be a good example. You intentionally punching a person in the face would be the very definition of an intentional tort. You are responsible for all the damages that were caused by your striking the other person. A word of caution: you cannot insure against an intentional tort, as it is against public policy. If you intentionally strike someone, you will be personally responsible for the damages. There will be no liability coverage to pay the damages.

Tort Reform

The civil justice system is rational. The occasional ridiculous verdict appears on the front page and the reversal, months later, appears hidden on the back page.

From 1986 to 2004, civil jury trials in Texas declined by 49%. Personal injury damage cases are less than ten percent of all cases filed. Texas residents were hoodwinked when they voted for tort reform in 2004, to stop a personal injury litigation crisis that literally did not exist. Well-meaning people were duped into tilting a civil justice system against themselves. No one thinks it will happen to them or their children, until it does.

The defense can now add defendants who are insolvent, or even unknown, to diminish the victim's recovery, without recourse. It is called submission of a responsible third party and it is why you need an exceptional lawyer to prevail in Texas in the post tort reform era.

CHAPTER 2

WHAT SHOULD I DO AT THE SCENE OF A SERIOUS COLLISION?

When someone is involved in an accident, the immediate decisions they make will have a lasting effect on the value of their case. I will share with you a hypothetical situation that is actually a conglomerate of many different cases I have handled in the real world.

Your friend, we will call him Bob, was just hit by an 18-wheeler and forced into a high impact collision with a freeway barrier. The crash really shook him up. He considers himself a good citizen and he was taught to be a stand-up guy. Bob tries to minimize what happened to him and he waves off the offer of an ambulance. The driver admits the accident was his fault and pleads with Bob not to call the police. Bob agrees and gets a ride home from a friend. The next day, he contacts the company's insurance carrier to file a claim. The adjuster asks, very casually, how Bob is doing.

Not wanting to appear like a whiner, Bob assures the adjuster that he is fine. The adjuster puts Bob at ease as they talk about sports. He shares with the adjuster that he played college football and is an avid hunter and outdoorsman. Bob gets the sense that the adjuster is a great guy and they are becoming friends. The adjuster totals Bob's car and sends him a check for his property damage immediately. This confirms Bob's suspicion that he did not really need a lawyer. Two days later, the nagging back pain has become unbearable and Bob cannot do his job like he did before. He takes over the counter pain medication and tries to get through it. He continues working in utter misery because he has bills to pay.

After two weeks of suffering, Bob finally breaks down and goes to a doctor. The doctor, fearing the worst, has an MRI performed, which shows Bob has two ruptured discs in his lower spine and needs a fusion. Bob does not have health insurance and the cost of a double fusion in Texas is $120,000. Bob pleads with his doctors and they agree to perform the operation for $80,000 cash up front. Bob was given a written estimate and he sends it to the insurance adjuster, along with the MRI and medical record from his doctors. This is where Bob is about to learn a hard lesson about the realities of a personal injury case.

When the adjuster declines to pay and offers Bob $5,000 to settle the claim, he threatens to get a lawyer, thinking that threat will bring the adjuster to his senses. He then offers to settle the whole claim for $60,000. Bob assumes his doctors will be as reasonable with him as he is being with the insurance carrier. Unfortunately, Bob is wrong. Bob is eventually forced to hire a personal injury attorney. He forgets to tell him about his dealings with the adjuster. The personal injury attorney contacts the carrier to inform them Bob has counsel. He then sends all the medical records with a demand for $300,000 to settle the claim. The adjuster responds that Bob did not get hurt in the accident.

The adjuster ticks off all his reasoning as follows: Bob refused an ambulance, he never went to the hospital, never missed work, was never treated, told the adjuster he was fine, and admitted to playing college football, which is where he must have injured his back. The adjuster also pulled up Bob's Facebook page and downloaded photos of Bob waterskiing and hiking. Just getting warmed up, the adjuster continues: before getting an attorney, Bob was willing to take $60,000, so the demand for $300,000 is lawyer-driven and Bob is a fake, just trying to get rich off the misfortune of others. In addition, the adjuster informs counsel he has interviewed their driver and it turns out the accident was Bob's fault. Wow! What did Bob do wrong? Basically, everything. Since you are reading this book, you will not be taken advantage of, like your friend Bob.

So, what should you do if you are involved in a serious accident? First, call the police and get an accident report filed by a police officer, so it is not your word against the other driver's. It does not matter if the driver orally admits fault. They can conveniently deny it later and call you a shameless liar. A police report will end any shenanigans by the defense when it comes to who is at fault.

Second, if you have been hit hard, accept the ambulance ride to the hospital. You are not a doctor and your adrenaline is flowing. Maybe you are hurt and the adrenaline has masked all the pain signals that are attempting to tell your brain you are seriously injured. Your failure to go by ambulance will be used by the other side to say it was not a serious accident. Otherwise, you would have gone to the hospital.

Third, when you are released from the hospital, go straight to a personal injury attorney. Do not use your divorce lawyer, family estate lawyer, or your company's corporate lawyer. I am sure they are good at what they do, but personal injury law is filled with landmines. You need a professional, especially in the era of tort reform.

Fourth, start medical treatment immediately. If the doctor gives you a prescription, fill it that same day. If you feel bad, call in sick.

Fifth, delete all social media. The other side will access it and find things to use against you. How do I know this? I always access the defendant's social media and use it against them. Be smart and remove any offensive photos or text messages from your cell phone. This includes jokes and political commentary. A jury consists of twelve strangers pulled at random. It is important not to offend them from the outset.

Sixth, do not ever speak with an adjuster without your attorney present. If the other side's insurance company tries to contact you, do not take the call. If you have answered the call, once they identify themselves, tell them you have an attorney and your attorney will call them. Do not have a conversation with them. Their sole purpose in talking with you is to try to diminish your case. They want to pay as little as possible. They are not looking out for your best interest. Nothing good can come from talking to them. Do not, for a minute, think you are smarter than them or you can manipulate them. They do this for a living.

Seventh, do not ever lie to your lawyer. He or she cannot protect you from things they are unaware of. This is so important I will say it twice. Do not ever lie to your lawyer. If you do, you have seriously wounded your case. Be honest with your doctor and only treat for as long as necessary. Get back to work as fast as you can, with due regard to your health.

I had a client who suffered a radical leg amputation, mid-thigh. He called me early on to inform me he had ruined his case. He had gotten back to work in only 90 days with a titanium rod for a leg. To make matters worse, so he thought, he was also given a raise by a very understanding boss. He had no future lost wages and he feared his economic damages would now be minimal. That young man is now a millionaire. Juries pay money to people they like and we all like people with character and guts. That kid had more courage than any ten people chosen at random. Hard workers receive something in the courtroom that is critical. It is called respect. Always do what your lawyer says. Turn off the news, get off the Internet, and stop talking to friends and family about your case. If you take these steps you are not guaranteed victory but you are already well ahead of the general public. Trust me when I say your lawyer will greatly appreciate the position he or she is in because you played it smart from the beginning.

CHAPTER 3

IMPORTANCE OF EVIDENCE IN A PERSONAL INJURY CASE

Witnesses and evidence are critical in a personal injury case. Photograph everything: the vehicles, your injuries, the hospital stay, and rehab. In a death case, family albums are critical to show a loving family. Video of family get-togethers, birthday and Mother's Day cards can really make the family relationship very real for a jury. If there is a serious injury, your MRIs, CAT scans, X-rays, and surgical photos are crucial. Nothing will enhance a case more than showing plates and screws holding your skeletal frame together.

All carriers will request a recorded statement. We never say no to the request because we have nothing to hide. You have to have your attorney at your side while making the statement. A good recorded statement makes a proper settlement much more likely. The statement can be used against the client in court, so it is a two-edged sword. A truly bad recorded statement makes litigation much more likely. Review the accident report before making the call, have a list of your injuries in front of you when making your statement. Keep it short and business-like with no chitchat.

Much of the evidence is obtained through what is called discovery. It consists of requests for production, interrogatories, requests for admissions, and depositions. A request for production will force the defendant to give you their documentation. Company emails are critical to show they had knowledge before a tragic accident and did nothing. Written company policies that the employees were unaware of and violated with alarming regularity will be sure to create anger amongst the jurors, who will then be charged with assessing damages. Interrogatories are written questions the other side must answer, in writing, and be sworn to before a notary.

The deposition is the most powerful discovery tool. You have the witnesses answering your questions under oath, on video. Many a case is lost when a company representative behaves badly in a videotaped disposition. The company is left no alternative but to settle, on your terms, to prevent the testimony from appearing in open court for the whole world to see.

Two quick examples. I had a company employee testify that the general manager confiscated his laptop computer and destroyed the evidence the day after my client had burned to death. In another case my client had died of heat exhaustion while working outside in 104 degree heat. The corporate representative blamed the victim for his own death. When asked why the deceased was at fault he stated on video, “I think he was dumb as hell.” You cannot make this up. I have countless anecdotes of this kind of damaging evidence, all on video.

Get Medical Attention Immediately After An Accident

When injured in an accident, getting prompt medical attention is critical. The longer you delay, no matter the reason, the less value is placed on your claim by an adjuster. They even have a term for it. They will tell your lawyer you have a "hole in treatment." The larger the hole, the less money will be offered.

You must do what the doctor instructs. Otherwise, they will put a note in your medical record that says you were non-compliant or left against medical advice. These terms will destroy your case.

Keep A Diary Of Events After An Accident

It is an excellent idea to keep a diary of what happened after the accident. It needs to include all the doctors you had to see, the pain you are in, and the sense of hopelessness and depression you experience. It can be very powerful when a grown man comes to tears while telling the jury his wife had to wipe him after going to the bathroom, because his arms were in casts. A detailed journal will make it easier to elicit this kind of testimony. Jurors are very sympathetic to a person suffering humiliation due to their injuries. It is compelling evidence of mental anguish.

Most people will not keep an accurate journal because they hate to write. If you are not inclined to write, leave it alone. A bad journal is worse than no journal at all and once you create a document, the other side can discover it.

Testimony versus Physical Evidence

I cannot emphasize enough how important evidence is to winning a personal injury case. While testimony from a party or family member is evidence, it is inherently suspect due to bias. If a person has a motive to lie, their testimony must be corroborated to be credible. We had a fatal accident involving an 18-wheeler where the driver claimed he did not see the plaintiff until the last second and he immediately applied his brakes but there was nothing he could do to avoid the collision. We obtained the black box from his rig.

We conclusively established with his own data recorder that he had visual site of the Plaintiff for 18 seconds before impact and then failed to brake for an additional 14 seconds after the impact. It was four in the morning and the driver had obviously fallen asleep. He failed to brake for 32 seconds from the time he could physically see the other vehicle. Without the physical evidence he might have gotten away with lying. After all, the only other witness (my client) was dead.

In another case involving catastrophic injuries delivered by a reckless 18-wheeler driver we took the position his driving logs were fabricated to comply with sleep requirements. The driver of course denied his logs were fraudulent and claimed they were completely accurate in every respect. He went so far as to say he would never lie in his driving logs. We obtained a year's worth of driving logs. We found an entry where he claimed to have made a trip from Dallas to Austin, Texas in 1.5 hours. Using simple math we calculated he had to average 160 MPH to get there that fast. I then accused him of driving 160 MPH based on his logs that we know are accurate because he assured us he would never lie. He responded that was impossible because there was a governor on the carburetor for his rig that would not let him go above 65MPH. He was so ignorant, he was not actually aware of how ridiculous he had become.

The defense cannot recover when they get caught lying on a galactic scale. This is the reason I tell my clients do not lie, ever. It is fatal when you get caught.

Statute Of Limitations For A Personal Injury Case

The statute of limitations for a personal injury case in Texas is two years. Be careful here because in some states you only have one year. When suing a governmental entity, there are other laws that require notice to the state in very specific ways. If you are dealing with a governmental entity in Texas, you must get to a lawyer immediately. You cannot depend on the two-year statute of limitations.

What Is A Comparative Negligence State?

Texas is a comparative negligence state. That means your negligence, if any, is deducted from the damage award. For example, if the jury awards $100,000 in damages and determines you were 40% negligent, then the $100,000 award is reduced by the judge and a judgment is entered for $60,000. If the plaintiff is found to have over 50% negligence then that is a complete bar to recovery. Using our same hypothetical $100,000 jury award, if the plaintiff was 51% negligent he is awarded nothing.

Why Is It Important To Buy Uninsured Motorist Coverage?

I often describe a personal injury case as a three-legged stool. You need liability, damages, and an entity that is able to pay. In most cases, the third leg is an insurance policy. If you remove one of the legs, the stool will not stand. No liability, no case. If no one did anything wrong, you have no one to hold responsible. If no damages occurred, then no case. Negligence does not translate to a money award if you are unhurt.

If a drunk, homeless man in a stolen car runs into you and cripples you for life, there is no case. He was negligent for driving drunk and your damages are enormous, but he is uninsured and lives under a bridge. You have no way of collecting anything from someone who literally has nothing.

It is very important to get uninsured motorist coverage with high limits and put a $1 million umbrella policy on top of it. Then, you cannot be victimized by the irresponsible, uninsured party.

CHAPTER 4

HOW LONG DOES A PERSONAL INJURY CASE TAKE TO SETTLE?

Your modest personal injury case can usually settle within 60 days of your being released from medical treatment. If you treat for two months from the time of your accident, you will probably have your case resolved in a total of four months. If you have massive damages that require litigation to resolve the matter, you are looking at one or two years.

The resolution options are straightforward. You file a claim and then follow up with documentation concerning medical bills, lost wages, photographs of the vehicles and injuries. You then engage in settlement discussions to try and come to an agreement. Most small cases settle here. Sometimes a large case will also settle here, but that is rare. This is many times the plaintiff's best day because attorney fees are at a minimum and expenses are virtually nonexistent. Not to mention the client is immediately compensated and avoids the emotional stress from litigation and countless delays.

If an agreement cannot be reached then suit is filed. Both sides go to war. During the course of discovery sometimes things look much worse for one side or the other and a settlement may be agreed to early on. Absent some dramatic reveal, the case will be mediated as trial draws near. It will take 6 months to 2 years to get there. If mediation fails then at the third trial setting after waiting for as much as 2 years you go to trial and get a verdict. Once the verdict is entered you may get the case resolved. Otherwise one side or the other files an appeal and the case languishes in appellate hell for an additional one to 2 years. If the court affirms your verdict then you get paid the actual amount on the judgement. If the case is reversed then you are back at square one waiting for your second jury trial. So why do defendants settle if they can engage in this kind of delay? The process is not free. Defendants are paying $600 an hour for defense lawyers to try and or appeal the lawsuit. It makes better economic sense for them to settle if the plaintiff is reasonable.

Our longest civil case lasted five years. At the end of five years the defendants settled with us for one million dollars. The defense costs were one million dollars. They could have settled early on and saved a million dollars in defense costs. That is why it makes economic sense for the defense to settle early on in many situations.

Many clients ask, "Will I do better if I try my case?" That is one of the most difficult questions. There is no easy answer. I turned down $5,000 on one case and a jury awarded $500,000. In another case I was offered $250,000 and did everything possible to convince my client to accept the offer. Long story short, he refused the offer and eventually got nothing. Trial is a throw of the dice. No one can ever guarantee you will get a better result at trial. Any lawyer who would be reckless enough to guarantee a result from a jury trial is either inexperienced or not very bright.

One of the most powerful tools available to a victim is the Stowers' Demand. A carrier owes their insured a duty of good faith. If a carrier has an opportunity to settle a case for their insurance limits, liability is clear, and the damages are well beyond their policy limits, they owe a duty to their insured to settle the case. If they refuse and the plaintiff gets a verdict above the insurance policy limits, then the defendant can sue his own insurance company for pushing him into bankruptcy for no good reason.

We send the Stowers Demand and give the carrier 30 days to tender their limits. We inform them, in writing, that this will be the only opportunity to settle for limits. If they refuse, we will try the case to verdict. In the event of an excess verdict, we will then sue them for the excess amount they unreasonably cost their insured. All the facts have to line up perfectly or there is no real threat. When the facts do line up, they will tender their limits in 30 days.

If the case requires a jury trial then it will take one to two years to get to trial in Texas. The US Justice Department shows the national average of civil cases tried to be 4%. The vast majority of cases will settle at mediation. I have published a book dealing exclusively with mediation titled "Mediation In A Personal Injury Case." I invite you to obtain a free copy on our website at Hamptonandrawlings.com. It goes into great detail as to what mediation is and how to prepare.

CHAPTER 5

DAMAGES THAT YOU CAN RECOVER IN A PERSONAL INJURY CASE

For a personal injury case, you may recover medical expenses (past and future), lost wages (past and future), pain and suffering, mental anguish, disfigurement, and disability. Each case is determined by its own unique facts. For a wrongful death case, spouses, children, and parents can recover for loss of consortium, loss of inheritance, loss of support, and loss of household services. For survival actions, the deceased's estate recovers funeral expenses, medical expenses, and conscious pain and suffering experienced by the deceased while dying.

It is important to note if the plaintiff suffers an immediate death then there is no recovery for conscious pain and suffering as there was none. Death was instant. The same result occurs if the plaintiff is knocked unconscious and then dies before regaining consciousness.

How Is the Worth Of A Personal Injury Case Determined?

The evaluation of the worth of a personal injury claim is very subjective. The first thing to compute is what are called hard damage, the economic loss that is able to be calculated. Other damages are called soft damages, because they cannot easily be reduced to a hard number.

There are companies that have stored all the jury verdicts going back for years. In order to find a value, you search the database for all verdicts with facts similar to your case. After acquiring 20 verdicts from the past few years, you throw out the lowest and the highest awards. You then average the remaining 18 verdicts and you now have a rough idea how your case will play out in front of a Texas jury.

My experience says case value is determined by the law and the facts surrounding each individual case. If you are demanding a ridiculous amount of money for a case, threatening litigation will not move the needle at all. They will invite you to file so they can crush you in front of a jury of your peers.

How Will A Carrier Try To Get Out Of Paying?

An insurance adjuster will use every trick in the book to avoid paying. They will insist that the plaintiff was at fault, or is not truly injured. They will drag out ancient injuries or criminal records to cast doubt on the injured party's credibility. They will hire corrupt doctors who will say the Plaintiff is not really hurt or the incident did not cause the injuries claimed. They will truly do anything it takes to avoid payment. When all else fails they try to interpret events in such a way that they can deny coverage and refuse to pay anything regardless of the facts and injuries.

A few real case examples should let the reader understand what is at stake. We had a case where a young lady was thrown from a golf cart and struck her head on the pavement causing permanent brain damage. Her medical ran over $100,000. The homeowners insurance carriers all denied coverage claiming homeowners insurance is exempt from an auto accident. Yes, a golf cart does have a motor, but under the definitions in the insurance contracts, it is a recreational vehicle and the exemption does not apply. Their auto policies supplied a total of $90,000 in coverage but the homeowners policies totaled $1,500,000 in coverage. We were able to defeat their denial of coverage and settled north of one million dollars.

An 18-wheeler struck and killed our client on a freeway at night. Our client's rear emergency lights were flashing red the entire time up to the moment of impact. He left a wife and nine children all under the age of 18. The insurance carrier hired an expert accident reconstruction team to fashion a defense. They drove the freeway at night while filming red tail lights on the freeway. The film that we were provided was very dark and the lights were hard to see. They claimed their driver could not see tail lights under these conditions.

Through discovery, we obtained several hours of video from the defense that included all footage from their reconstruction team. I sat through six hours of video and found the original footage where the lights appeared bright and easily seen. After filming this, the so-called experts pulled off the road, put a dark filter on the camera to obscure everything and then redid the filming. I heard one of them, off camera, exclaim, "that's much better!" I then heard several of them actually chuckle. We were originally provided only the altered footage. They tried to do this to a widow with nine minor children. We obtained enough funds to put mom in a six bedroom home and all nine children received college funds. Do you see how important evidence is when millions are at stake?

We represented a man who had his foot crushed when it got caught under the augur of a post hole digger. The employer denied knowing who the man was and the carrier offered zero claiming our client was a fraud. I hired the chief of police from a nearby small town to investigate the case (not wanting to be involved in a fraud). He went to the employer in his police uniform carrying a clipboard and demanded to know the whereabouts of Mr. Garcia (not his real name). The officer was wired the entire time.

We heard the employer ask if Mr. Garcia was wanted for a crime. The officer said he could not give out that information but he was looking for him. The employer retrieved Mr. Garcia's employee file and gave the officer his address. He also volunteered that the guy had faked an injury so they hoped he would be deported so they would not have to pay.

At the mediation I let defense counsel go first. He lectured us about honesty and excoriated us for trying to perpetuate a fraud. "The employer had never even heard of Mr. Garcia," insisted defense counsel. I winked at the mediator and said, "I am going to waive my opening argument and just play this tape of the employer." The defense lawyer came apart like a cheap suit. Seeing definitively that the employer was a lying fraud trying to cheat an honest man, they instantly tendered their policy limits. In private the mediator confided that was one of the best times he ever had at a mediation.

I do not want to give the impression that all adjusters and defense lawyers are a bunch of liars. Most are ethical and play by the rules. After 39 years in litigation, I unfortunately have way too many anecdotes like this.

CHAPTER 6

INDEPENDENT MEDICAL EXAM

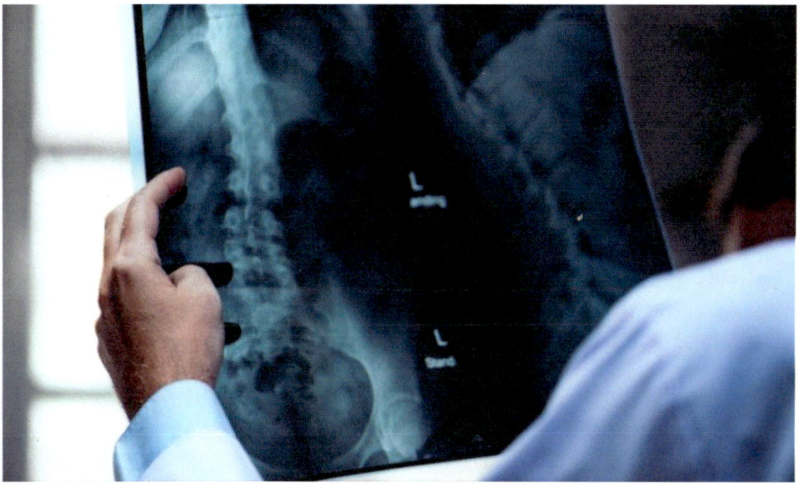

In any litigation where a plaintiff is claiming medical injuries, the defense is entitled to what is called an Independent Medical Exam (IME). The defense hires a doctor of their choosing, who they pay to review the plaintiff's medical records and perform an examination. The term "independent" is a misnomer. There is nothing independent about it. There are known "defense doctors" who are complete frauds. There is no doctor-patient relationship, no right to confidentiality, and the IME doctor cannot be sued for malpractice, no matter how outrageous his diagnosis may be.

As you might expect, the vast majority of these reports claim the plaintiff is not injured, or at least not as injured as he claims. They will always find a preexisting injury to blame for your discomfort or claim the collision was incapable of causing the plaintiff's injuries. Some of these doctors only testify for the defense and have been paid millions of dollars over the years to testify for insurance companies.

We represented a young lady who was struck by a wrecker that drove into the lobby of a tire store. The defense hired a doctor to say she did not have a serious head injury because the impact was not sufficient to cause the injuries we were claiming. I had a photo of the front of the wrecker with a huge shank of my clients blonde hair stuck to the crumpled hood. I also had a photo of the chair she was sitting in when this happened. Unfortunately for the insurance carrier, the chair was out in the parking lot with pooled blood all around it. The shattered window showed the violence that occurred when she was launched through the air on impact and landed in the parking lot. I guess they forgot to show their good doctor the scene photos before he wrote his "independent" medical opinion.

They sometimes watch you through a one way mirror before entering the room to see if you limp, or show signs of being able to move normally. Then when they are in the room they claim the plaintiff acted as though he was injured and is clearly faking. Since they record nothing you are at their mercy.

One doctor was so dishonest that I got a court order requiring the IME to be videotaped in its entirety by my camera crew. What could possibly be wrong with filming the IME? The doctor has nothing to hide, right. I mean after all, he is a doctor, right. This practitioner of the healing arts refused to see my client and the defense had to declare a different doctor to perform the IME. He would not allow himself to be videotaped while performing an examination.

I had another IME doctor who claimed my client did not have a serious back injury. This was an auto pedestrian collision where my client was literally knocked out of his shoes when struck by a car. He had chronic back pain from that day on. When cross examining the doctor, in front of a jury, it came out that he specialized in acupuncture. I confronted him with his own literature he published where he claimed he could cure all kinds of maladies by sticking a needle in your head. He had no specialty with the human spine but he felt quite comfortable rendering opinions to try and destroy the man's case.

The IME is a necessary evil in our system to maintain balance. In Texas, a person can record his or her own conversations without the consent of the other person. For people who are not in Texas a word of caution. In some states it is against the law to record a conversation without informing the other person you are doing so. Each state has its own penal code. You need to consult an attorney in your state before recording a conversation without someone's knowledge. In Texas, having your cell phone on record while being interviewed is one way to protect yourself. Make sure you are prepared before meeting with the other side's doctor.

CHAPTER 7

DO PRE-EXISTING INJURIES AFFECT A DAMAGES CLAIM?

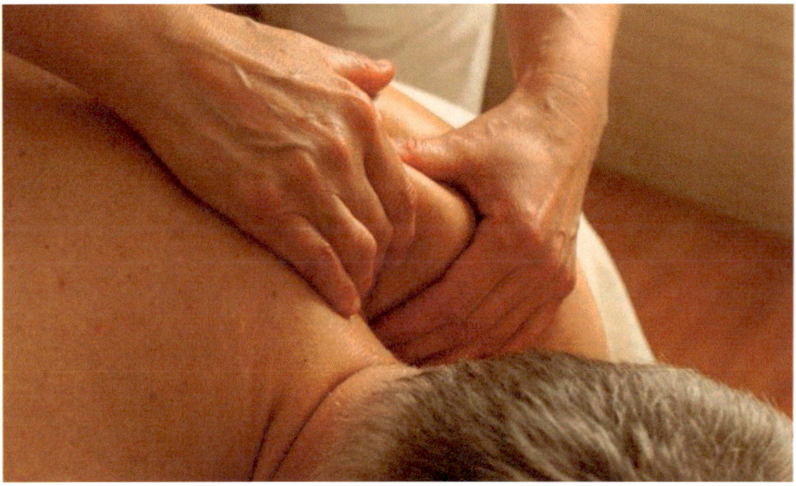

Prior to being involved in a catastrophic accident, most normal people have suffered some kind of injury while growing up. If you broke your arm as a child but break your ankle in an accident, that prior injury should be irrelevant. Most adjusters will try to use it to reduce the damages for your broken ankle. A good lawyer will push through that nonsense, but that is the reality of the civil litigation environment. What if you tore your medial meniscus in a football injury and now have a torn medial meniscus in the same knee, years later, from a car accident? Logic and fundamental fairness would dictate that if it was addressed and cured several years ago, it should have nothing to do with the new injury.

Fairness and logic, unfortunately, are not a priority of most insurance adjusters. They will claim they do not owe anything because the injury was preexisting. While a carrier legally does not have to pay for a preexisting injury, exacerbation of a preexisting injury is recoverable. If someone has suffered back pain for years and is hit from behind, causing the pain to increase, that increase in pain is a damage. Defense doctors are notorious for claiming the plaintiff's spinal injury was preexisting and not caused by the accident.

CHAPTER 8

BEWARE OF PREDATORY LENDERS

There is a shameful industry that will lend money on a personal injury case and charge you obscene amounts of interest. They get around the usury statutes by giving loans with no recourse. What that means is if you do not recover on your personal injury case, they do not get their money back. If you do recover, they get huge amounts of your settlement.

I kept a client from borrowing $10,000 against his case on one occasion. At time of settlement, they would have been entitled to $53,000. A bank loan at 7% would have cost him $700. If he had put that same $10,000 on a credit card, at 24% interest, he would have paid $2,400. For them to receive $53,000 for a $10,000 loan he had for a little over a year is outrageous. They would have gotten the equivalent of roughly a 430% return on their money. Do not borrow from this predatory system, ever.

On all our large recoveries, we insist the client put their money in a tax free annuity that guarantees them an income for life. To just hand someone a million dollars will only end in heartache. Everyone thinks they are different. Everyone thinks they are too smart to lose their money the way everyone else did. I have never seen anyone receive a large award, lump sum, that they did not eventually lose. The financial people joke that with an annuity "you can only go broke one month at a time."

There is another group of predators who prey on people with annuities. They pay you a lump sum for your annuity. Now you are getting about 66 cents on the dollar and have no protection. These people who abuse victims in such a calloused way have no soul. Once you lose your money, there is no going back. You cannot sue these predators because you made a bad decision.

CHAPTER 9

WHY IS IT CRITICAL TO HIRE AN ATTORNEY TO REPRESENT YOU?

The insurance industry claims they do not treat people any differently with or without an attorney. They are fair to everyone and analyze the value of each claim based on its merits, regardless of who is involved. This is patently false. Of course it makes a difference if you have a trained advocate. Do not show up to a gunfight with a clenched fist. It will end badly for you.

An attorney's trial and negotiating skills are critical to achieve maximum results on a claim. The difference between a good lawyer and a great lawyer is not much. The difference between a good lawyer and a bad lawyer is as wide as the Grand Canyon. Real lawyers do not need to say they are tough. It shows in their work.

After 28 years of handling personal injury cases, there is nothing corporate America could try and pull in a courtroom that would shock me in the least. A true story. Jason (not his real name) was an iron worker, twenty feet in the air, straddling an iron girder that was being connected to a column on a massive construction site. The column had not been secured to the concrete pedestal properly and the entire column and iron beam tipped to the side. Jason was thrown off the girder and fell feet first to the ground below. His knee blew out the back of his leg and the side of his face was crushed. A life flight helicopter airlifted Jason to a trauma hospital that saved his life. While enroute he was given a sedative to calm him down. Upon arrival at the hospital they drew his blood to perform an immediate drug screen before giving him powerful sedatives and painkillers.

All the companies involved refused to pay Jason a dime. They all claimed they did nothing wrong. While I can understand a company trying to avoid responsibility for an injured worker when it is not their fault, what happened in this case was outrageous. They tried to blame Jason and fabricated evidence to destroy any chance he would have at obtaining economic justice for all he had lost. During depositions one coworker said he saw him smoking marijuana on the job site prior to falling off the beam. Another coworker testified under oath that Jason had told him that morning that he had taken methamphetamine. Both workers also said he had not hooked his safety line to his harness. One described the harness as orange nylon, and the other worker described it as a beige nylon harness. They each claimed both clips on his lanyard were fastened to the same D ring on his belt. They both claimed they had a specific memory of seeing the D ring on his harness. Jason's harness, which was removed from him at the scene, before he was loaded on the air ambulance, disappeared from the job site, never to be seen again.

The insurance company defense lawyers pontificated about personal responsibility. They claimed Jason's brutal injuries were the result of his own carelessness for not tying off and his irresponsible drug abuse. While this made things look grim for Jason, there was some additional evidence that I brought to the forefront. Jason's drug screen at the ER was positive for the sedative they gave him on the helicopter, but negative for any other kind of drug. They screened for methamphetamine and marijuana and he was negative on both. We know the test was valid because it had a positive for the sedative they gave him on the helicopter.

I also had a photograph of Jason up on the steel at another job. Jason was an amateur cowboy and leather worker. Jason had made his own harness out of dark brown leather. He never owned a harness that was orange or beige nor made of nylon. The belt that wrapped around his waist was 4 inch wide leather. There were no D rings in his belt at all. When a worker is threatened with his job, it becomes easy to say things that your employer wants to hear, regardless of the truth. Without the photos and the hospital lab report, Jason would have been at the mercy of these ruthless individuals. Jason's leg was eventually amputated and he had permanent brain damage. His case eventually settled for a confidential amount and I put his funds in a structure so Jason received a monthly check. He would be taken care of for the rest of his life. This, unfortunately, is the day-to-day reality when suing corporate America for large sums of money.

Anyone, no matter how poor, can afford the best personal injury attorneys in the business. This is made possible by contingency fee contracts. When we take a case, we are paid a percentage of what we win for the client. In large cases involving complex litigation, we charge 40% of what we recover. We also pay for all litigation expenses upfront, with the understanding we will recover our costs from the settlement. The client does not have to pay out-of-pocket during the course of litigation. If the case is lost, then we are paid nothing for our time and we do not get our expenses back. We only get paid if we win.

You are not required to have an attorney to handle your case, but only an idiot would litigate without one. Handling a personal injury case without a lawyer is like performing your own surgery. Not a good idea because no matter how simple it may look from the outside, there are a million things that can go wrong. The differences between trial and mediation are stark.

In trial you pick a jury of 12 people chosen at random to hear the case and render a decision. Trial is war. You present your evidence while the other side tries to minimize or undo what you are trying to prove. Then the defense puts on their evidence while you try to minimize or undue everything they are presenting. To call it adversarial is an understatement. The jury is not just judging the evidence. They are judging the lawyers as well. Every move, every question and response, another opportunity to save the day or blow it. If you truly understand litigation, the stress is enormous.

I laugh when lawyers claim they are not nervous in trial. For that to be true they either do not know what they are doing or they are liars. Every mentor I have had who was a lion in the courtroom always admitted to being nervous before the trial would actually start.

I will share a true case example. A car fell off a jack, in a garage, and injured a mechanic. The adjuster came out to the shop, inspected the scene, and spoke with the injured man. He wrote him a $20,000 check on the spot. This man bragged to his friends about how he "didn't need a lawyer and got to keep all his money." Unfortunately, our hard working mechanic had no health insurance. When his back pain did not go away, he finally went to a doctor. He had a ruptured disc in his back and needed surgery. It would cost over $100,000.

He came to my office to hire me to represent him. We immediately called the insurance carrier to open a claim for him. They informed us the case had already been settled for $20,000 and the client had signed a release. When we confronted him with these facts, he admitted he took $20,000 and signed the release, but claimed he did not read the release, so it was not valid. Wrong. I will never forget the look of disbelief on his face when we refused his case. He had settled a possible $500,000 fusion case for $20,000.

The law and the facts determine the value of a case. If you are untrained in the law, you will not be able to assess the value of a claim other than to make a wild guess. As Abe Lincoln said, "A man who represents himself has a fool for a client."

CHAPTER 10

HOW IS HAMPTON & RAWLINGS DIFFERENT FROM OTHER FIRMS?

HAMPTON &
RAWLINGS

PERSONAL INJURY ATTORNEYS

Hampton & Rawlings predominately handles personal injury cases. We have successfully prosecuted numerous 18-wheeler and auto accidents, home fires, train derailment, ATV rollovers, bus fatalities, and product defect cases to name a few. Since 1991 we have resolved well over one thousand cases. We screen our cases closely and stay current on the law, which is why we seldom lose. I prefer to work on serious cases involving brain damage, amputation, or death. The devastating effect these cases have on a family is enormous. They deserve an attorney that will take these problems on as if they were his or her own.

Creativity, honesty and courage is what sets us apart. We are constantly looking for effective ways to make our cases come alive, to make the other side feel the fear and horror that our clients were forced to endure by the careless and the downright malicious. We have a medical illustrator who renders the scans and X-rays in color and 3D so they convey the true horror of what lies beneath the skin. We use professional photographers to capture scars on film in vivid color.

We have a studio that creates our media and power point presentations to allow us to give gripping presentations at mediation or trial. We video tape our depositions so the animators are able to edit the video so the jury is hearing the witness testimony along with our arguments. It prevents our opponents from misstating the evidence or accusing us of manufacturing things. It allows us to own the room.

For example, I once put on an animation for a case that involved a man who had died of mechanical asphyxiation after being pinned underneath a heavy-duty truck. Unable to expand his lungs due to the way in which he was trapped by the truck, he literally drowned in the air. The exhibit was an animation that depicted a human frame enclosing the circulatory system, and included the sound of a beating heart. There was a time clock in the upper left corner that was running down to zero while the blood was turning from red to blue, and a classic heart monitor graph on the top right that showed each heartbeat. As the audible sound of the heartbeat began to slow and the blood was turning blue, the clock eventually hit zero, the heart monitor flatlined, and the alarm sounded. It made our client's death become real for everyone in that room.

Another example involved a bar that was notorious for overserving patrons. One of them struck our client in a cross walk in an auto pedestrian collision causing her to have permanent brain damage. We sent a camera crew into the bar before filing suit and got footage of a man passed out at the bar, people throwing up in the bathroom and a drunk couple having sex on a pool table. Not completely satisfied because I knew they would lie and claim they do not overserve their patrons, I sent the crew in a second time and they filmed their fellow investigator while he drank 7 shots and 4 mixed drinks in one sitting at the bar before leaving. Eleven drinks in a little over an hour rendered him smashed out of his mind. No one tried to stop him from leaving in that condition. During the owner's deposition he denied his employees would ever overserve a patron. We then put the videos on screen and forced him to identify every one of his employees on film. That case would not have settled without actual footage to expose them as liars.

We have access to a safety firm that does accident recreation with very realistic animation. Every year it gets better and better. In the near future it will be as good as actual video. They use the physical evidence coupled with witness testimony to show the accident as it actually occurred.

We instruct our clients to always, always, always tell the truth, no matter how bad it may hurt the case. While some facts may hurt the value of the case, lying is fatal. We assume our opponent is a diabolical genius who knows everything about our case. Your credibility is everything.

The real litigators understand this. The pretenders think they are smart enough to lie their way around bad facts. Real lawyers know there is no perfect case and deal with bad fact as best they can. Every time I catch the defense lying it is a good day for the plaintiff.

In one case during jury selection I promised the jury I would tell the truth throughout the trial. I invited them to punish us severely if any of our witnesses lied. "If my side lies, give us nothing, because that is what liars deserve." I then said "of course fairness would dictate that if the other side lies, well, you know what to do." I already knew the defense was going to lie and I could prove it.

I had demanded $50,000 on the case. The offer from the defense was $15,000. I caught the defendant and the defense attorney both lying during the course of the trial. The jury award was $175,000. Several jurors told me afterward the contrast between the two sides made them want to give me more than they did but some jurors were too stingy to really give the defense what they deserved for being so dishonest.

Courage is hard to measure or prove. When I speak of courage, I mean an ability to act in difficult situations. While in the Harris County District Attorneys Office, I had my life seriously threatened on three different occasions. Two defendants were charged with murder and one was an armed bank robber. My family had an evacuation plan, should they ever get the call to get out. I kept those three files on my desk and worked them every day. Two of those defendants ended up with life sentences and the third received 85 years in prison. The thought of handing the case off to someone else never entered my mind.

When I transitioned to civil law and some posturing insurance defense attorney would suggest I did not have the guts to try a civil case, I would laugh. I have yet to have an insurance adjuster threaten to kill me and wipe out my family. As a reminder, I carry a photo in my brief case of me skydiving. When things get rough, I pull out the photo to remind myself I have seen scarier.

Last July, I ran with the bulls in Pamplona, Spain. A man who will jump out of a perfectly good airplane or square off with a two-ton bull cannot be intimidated by some guy in a suit. My law partner was a bouncer in a west Texas beer joint while in law school. He brawled with drunk bikers and cowboys on a regular basis. He is just as tough, if not more so.

So, now is a good time to review. If you are in an accident you need to call the police to the scene and then see a doctor immediately. Follow your doctor's instructions meticulously. Hire an attorney as soon as possible. Do not ever lie to your doctor or your lawyer. Document everything with written records or photographs and video. Do not speak to the other side. Take down all social media. (You can always put it back up when the case is over.) Do not tell people about your case. Ignore well-meaning advice from non-lawyers. Get back to work, if possible, quickly and demonstrate courage. Cooperate with your lawyer and be sure to tell him or her everything. If you do all these things, you will be head and shoulders above most who make mistakes in how they approach a litigation environment.

When mentoring young lawyers I caution them that no case is worth more than the Plaintiff. If the Plaintiff is worthless, then so is your case. Jurors give the big awards to people they like and respect. Show humility and be humble throughout the process. It will pay huge dividends in the long run.

While the system is not perfect, I promise you the system is rational. If you find yourself in personal injury litigation, stay strong, show humility, and be brave. Make sure your attorney is experienced in personal injury. Your life is being decided in that courtroom. You will be the one to decide if you will be a victim or a victor, regardless of the outcome. I wish each one of you the best of luck.

INDEX

NOTES

Made in the USA
Monee, IL
05 November 2026

67385054R00045